AF225725

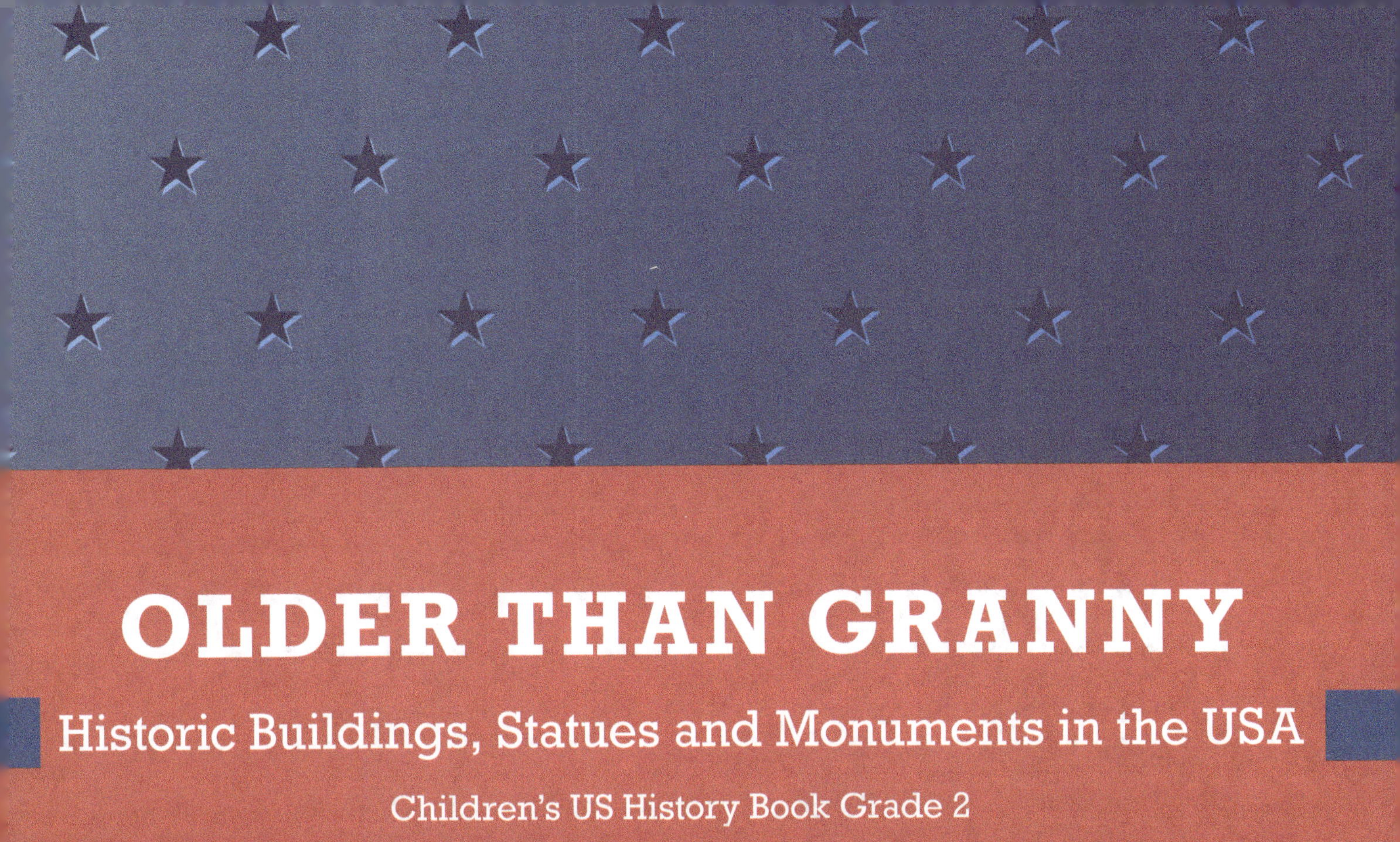

OLDER THAN GRANNY

Historic Buildings, Statues and Monuments in the USA

Children's US History Book Grade 2

First Edition, 2024

Published in the United States by Speedy Publishing LLC, 40 E Main Street, Newark, Delaware 19711 USA.

© 2024 Baby Professor Books, an imprint of Speedy Publishing LLC

Baby Professor Books are available at special discounts when purchased in bulk for industrial and sales-promotional use. For details contact our Special Sales Team at Speedy Publishing LLC, 40 E Main Street, Newark, Delaware 19711 USA. Telephone (888) 248-4521 Fax: (210) 519-4043.

10 9 8 7 6 * 5 4 3 2 1

Print Edition: 9781541987470

Digital Edition: 9781541987869
Hardcover Edition: 9781541998223

See the world in pictures. Build your knowledge in style.
www.speedypublishing.com

TABLE OF CONTENTS

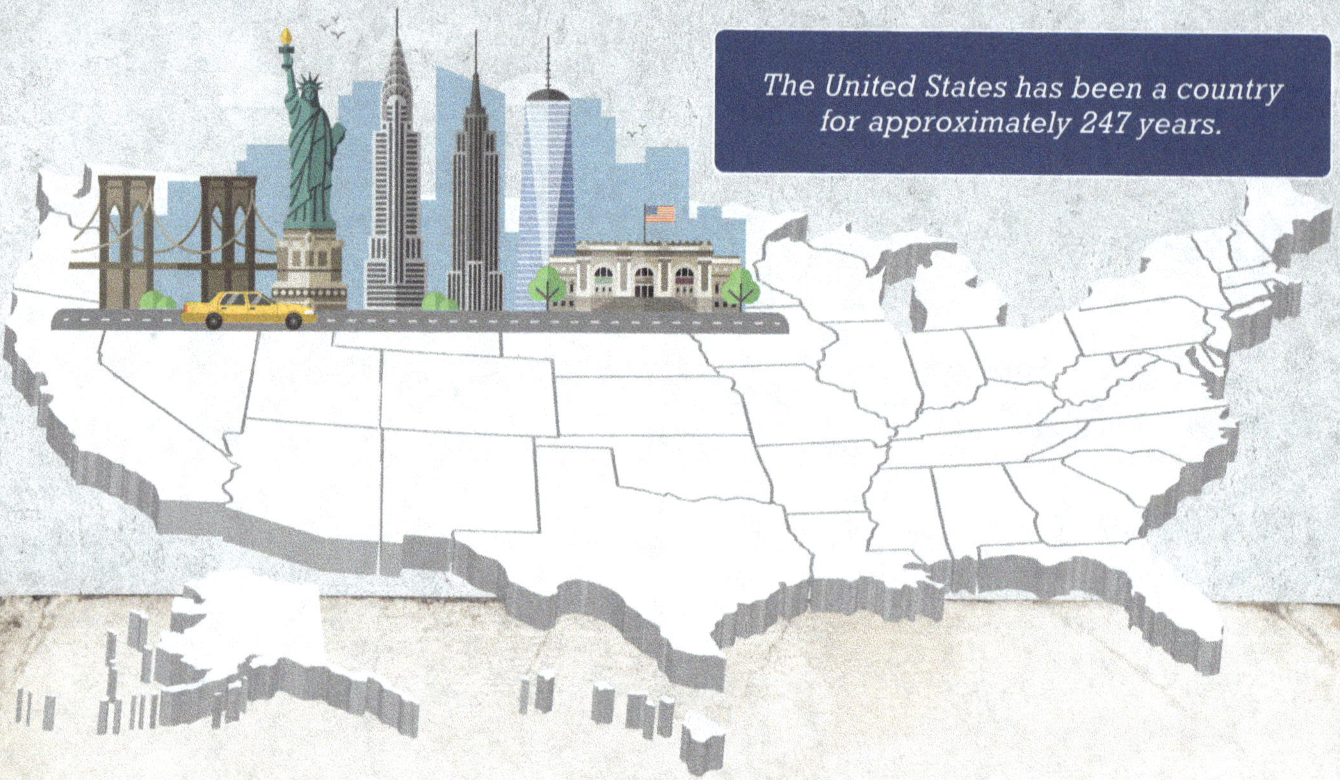

The United States has been a country for approximately 247 years.

The United States has been a country for less than three hundred years. That might seem like a long time. For a country though, it is not long. There are some countries that are thousands of years old! The United States became a country when they declared independence from Britain. Today, there are many buildings, statues, and monuments to remember this event.

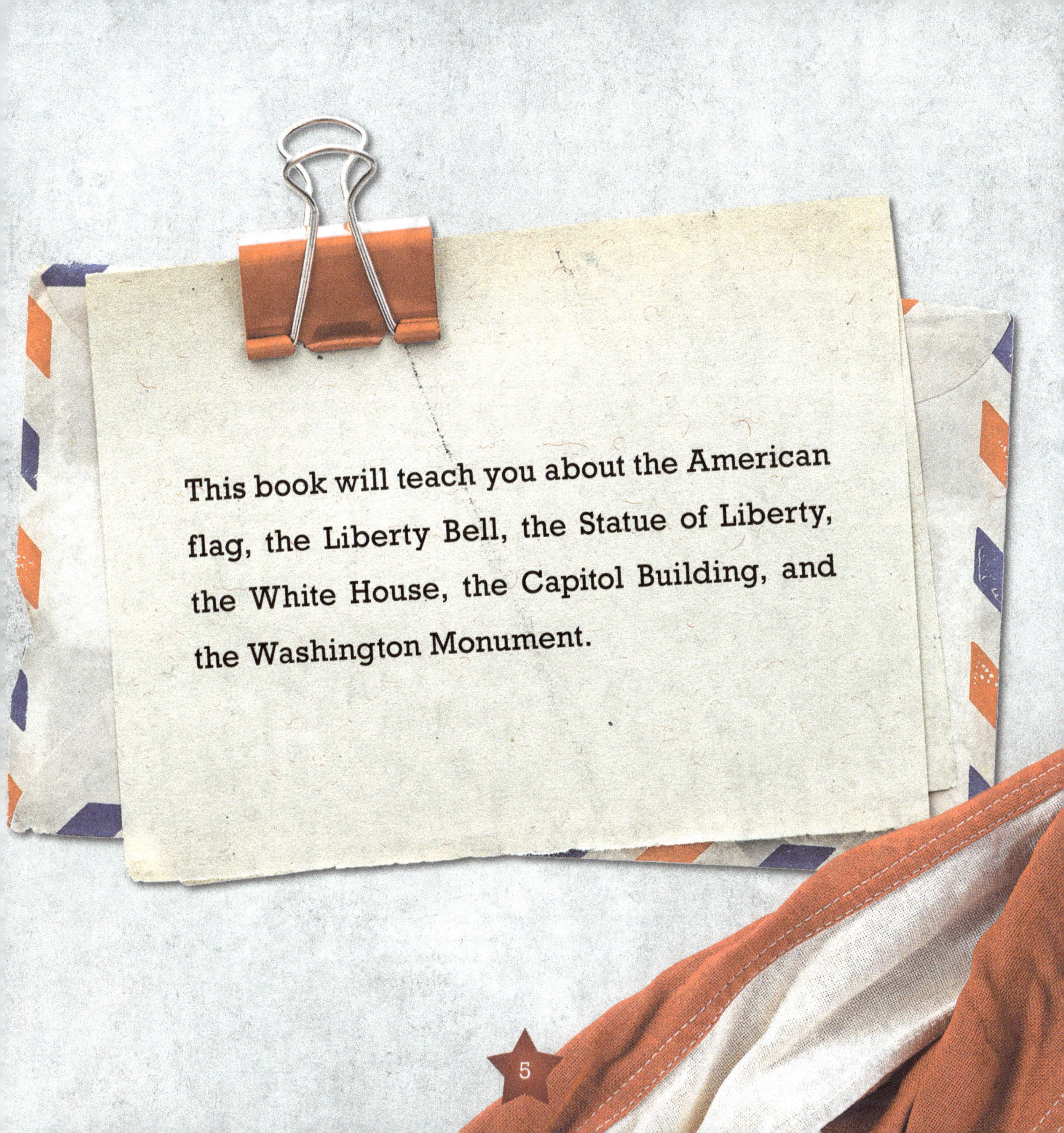

This book will teach you about the American flag, the Liberty Bell, the Statue of Liberty, the White House, the Capitol Building, and the Washington Monument.

CHAPTER ONE
BECOMING A FREE
COUNTRY

All countries have a flag. The country's flag is supposed to be a symbol. It should be a symbol for the country and what it stands for. The American flag is sometimes called Old Glory or the Stars and Stripes.

The flag for the United States of America has red and white stripes across. There are seven red stripes and six white. These are for the thirteen original colonies that founded the United States of America. The flag also has white stars on a blue canton. This canton is on the top left of the flag. There are fifty stars for each of the fifty states.

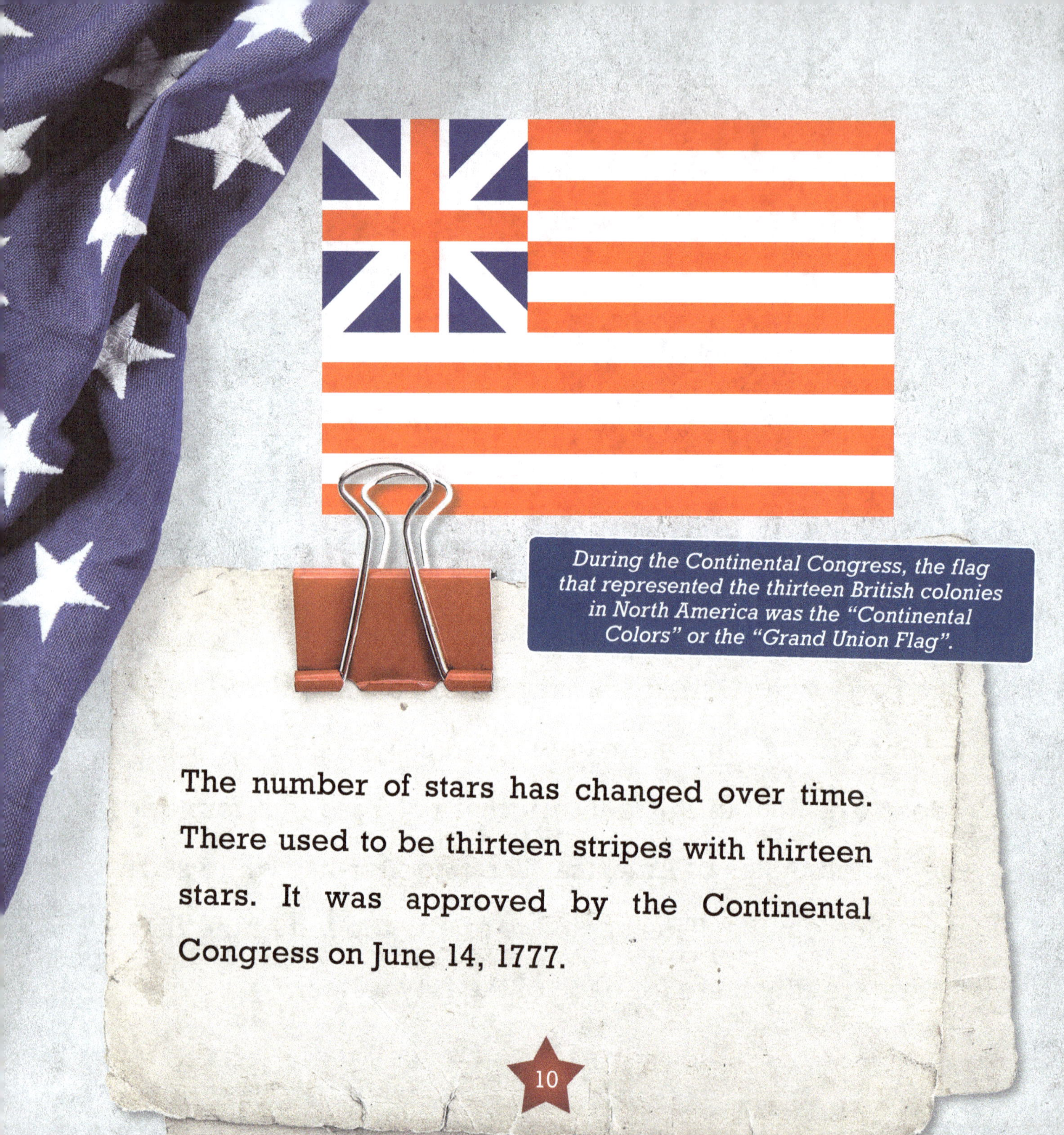

The number of stars has changed over time. There used to be thirteen stripes with thirteen stars. It was approved by the Continental Congress on June 14, 1777.

Later, a star and stripe was added for each new state. In 1818, it was decided to change that. From now on, the stripes would represent the first thirteen colonies. The stars would match the number of states.

US Flag with 20 stars and 13 stripes

Our current flag has existed since 1960. According to legend, it was Betsy Ross who sewed the first flag.

General George Washington, Major George Ross, Robert Morris, and Betsy Ross with the first American flag, approved by Congress on June 14, 1777

DID YOU KNOW?

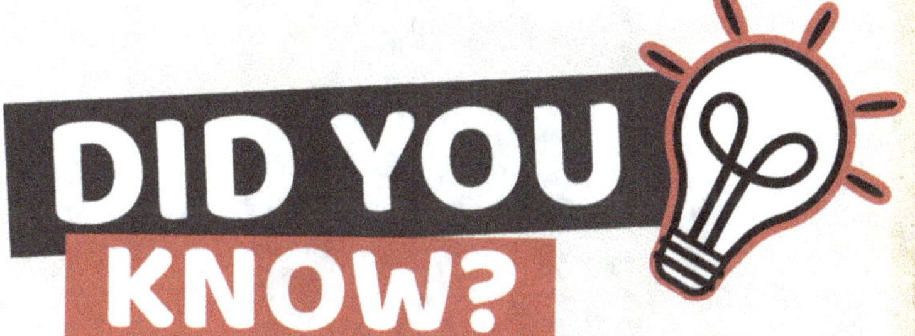

Elizabeth Griscom was born on January 1, 1752, in Philadelphia, Pennsylvania. She was known as Betsy. She married John Ross in 1773. They both worked in the upholstery business John started. Upholstery is the soft padding that covers furniture. John Ross died in 1776, the same year Betsy might have sewn the first American flag.

John Ross

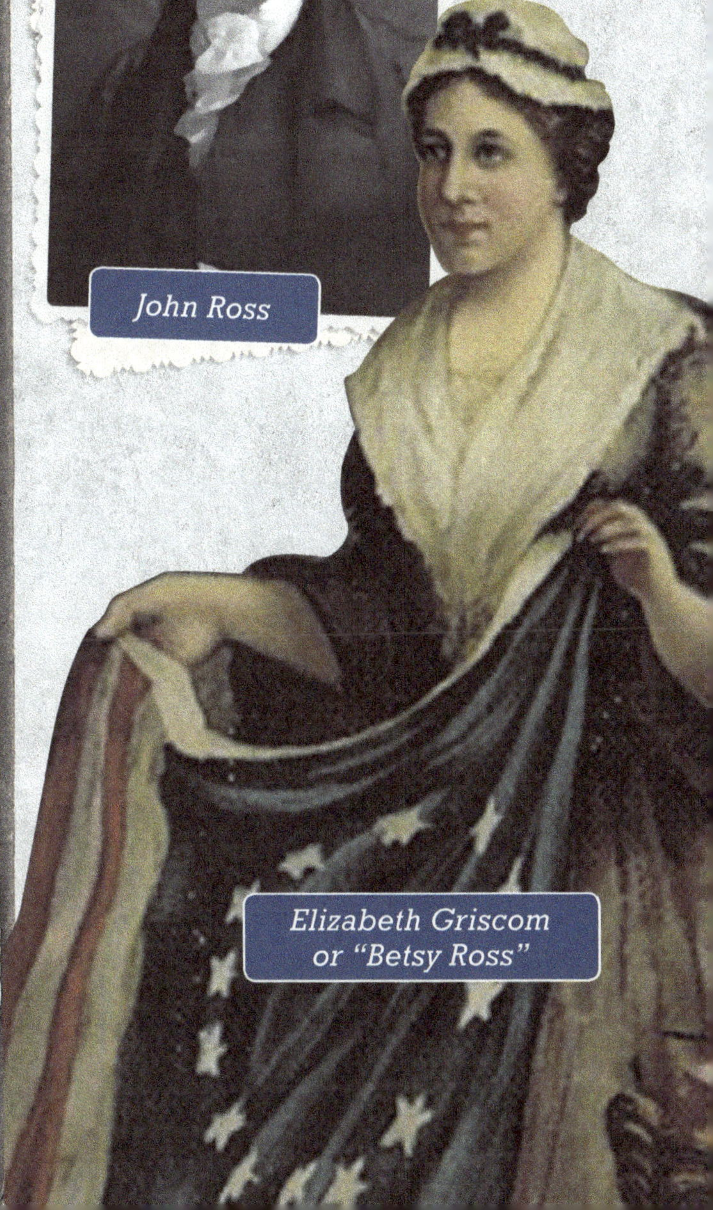

Elizabeth Griscom or "Betsy Ross"

The flag for the United States also inspired the national anthem. It was written by Francis Scott Key. It was during the war of 1812. Key saw the flag still flying in a fort that survived an attack.

The Liberty Bell was rung in 1776 in Philadelphia. It was rung to celebrate the United States' independence from Britain. It was not called the Liberty Bell until 1839. It was named by enslaved people who wanted liberty, in other words, freedom.

The Liberty Bell

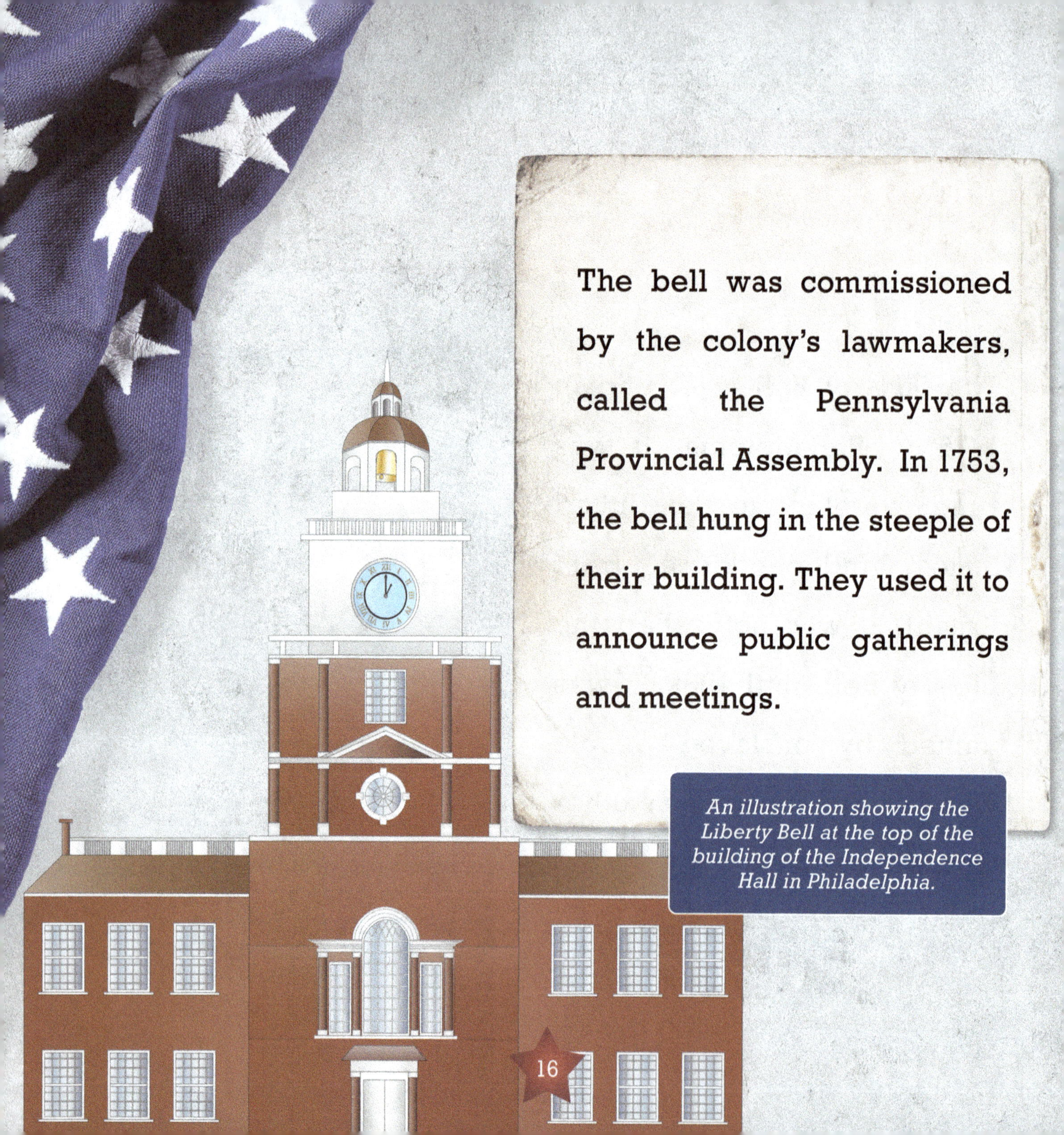

The bell was commissioned by the colony's lawmakers, called the Pennsylvania Provincial Assembly. In 1753, the bell hung in the steeple of their building. They used it to announce public gatherings and meetings.

An illustration showing the Liberty Bell at the top of the building of the Independence Hall in Philadelphia.

16

The bell was rung when the Declaration of Independence was read publicly. This was on July 8, 1776. Patriots hid the bell during the American Revolution. They were afraid the British soldiers would melt it for cannonballs.

The Liberty Bell was hidden in Allentown for nine months until its June 27, 1778 return to Philadelphia

The bell went back to the assembly building when the war was over. The building was also renamed. It is now Independence Hall.

The bell is not there now though. The bell became cracked in 1835. This was likely during the funeral of Chief Justice John Marshall. In 1846, the crack became bigger. No one has rung it since then and in 2003 the bell was moved. Now it is in a building named the Liberty Bell Center. It is near Independence Hall.

The Liberty Bell Center, Independence National Historical Park, Philadelphia

DID YOU KNOW?

Did you know? John Marshall was the fourth chief justice in the U.S. Supreme Court. That made him the highest ranking judge in the United States. Marshall helped shape the Supreme Court. The Supreme Court was recognized as being able to decide if laws were constitutional. The constitution shows the laws and values America is founded on.

John Marshall

John Marshall, Philadelphia Museum of Art

21

THROUGHOUT ALL THE LAND UNTO A
EMBLY OF THE PROVINCE OF PENSEL
22

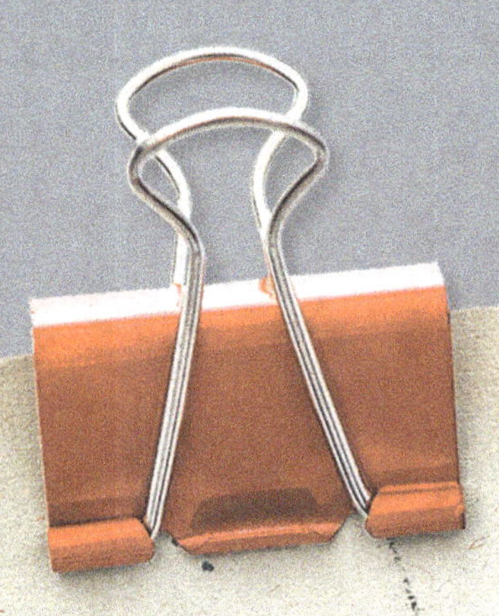

The Liberty Bell is about three feet tall and twelve feet wide at the bottom. It is mostly made of tin and copper. On the bottom of the bell is a verse from the Bible. It says "Proclaim liberty throughout all the land unto all the inhabitants thereof." It is from the book of Leviticus, chapter 25, verse 10.

THE STATUE OF LIBERTY

The Statue of Libery in New York City

The Statue of Liberty has been in New York since 1886. Its proper name is *Liberty Enlightening the World*. The light comes from the flame she carries. Liberty is shown as a woman with a crown. The statue is on Liberty Island. This is not far from Manhattan Island. It is just off the southern tip.

26

The statue is about 151 feet high. It also has a concrete base. Including the base, it is 305 feet high! The statue is made of an iron framework. This framework is covered in sheets of pounded copper.

The Statue of Liberty is one of the highest statues in the world, and is an iconic symbol of freedom and democracy.

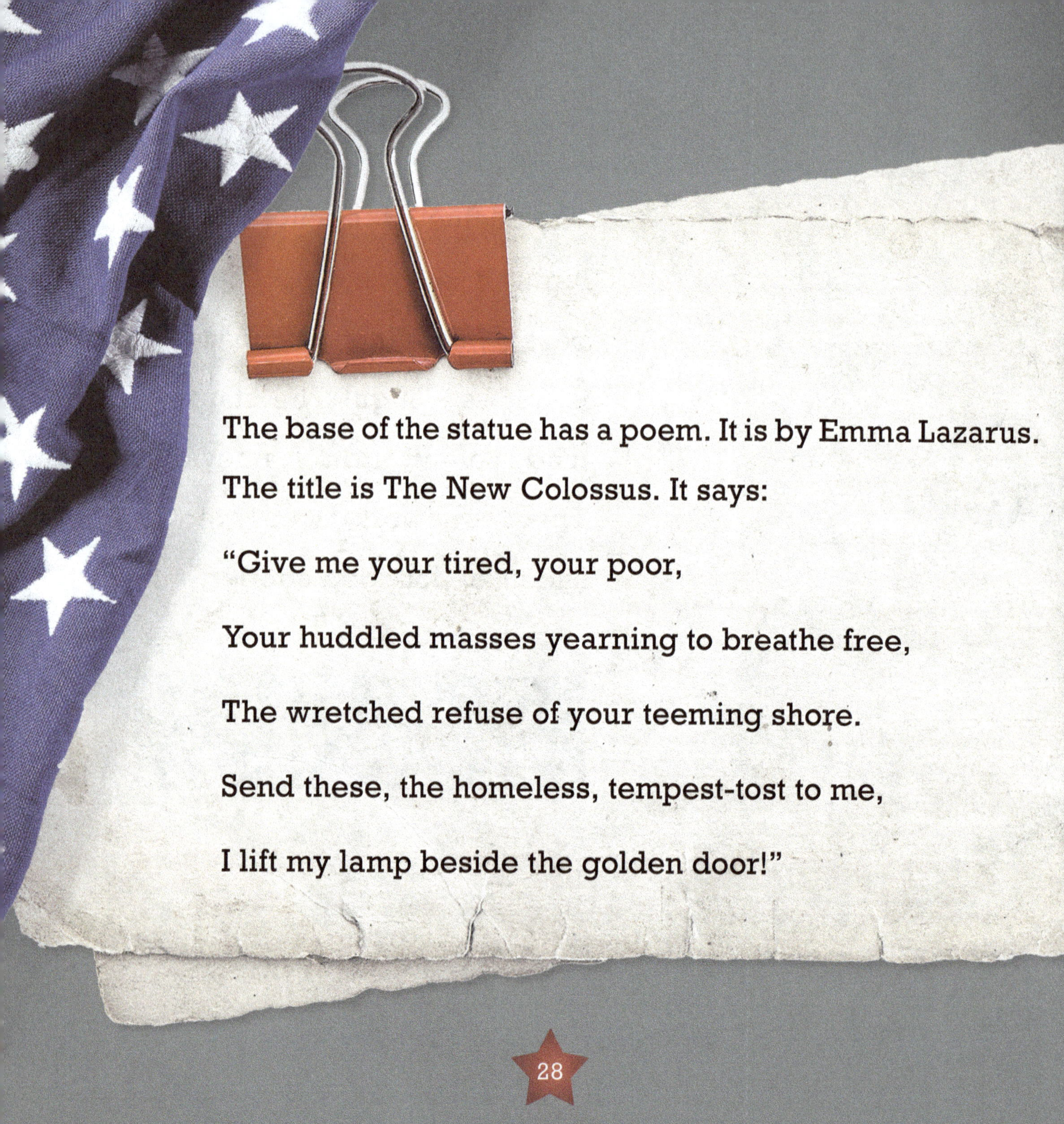

The base of the statue has a poem. It is by Emma Lazarus.

The title is The New Colossus. It says:

"Give me your tired, your poor,

Your huddled masses yearning to breathe free,

The wretched refuse of your teeming shore.

Send these, the homeless, tempest-tost to me,

I lift my lamp beside the golden door!"

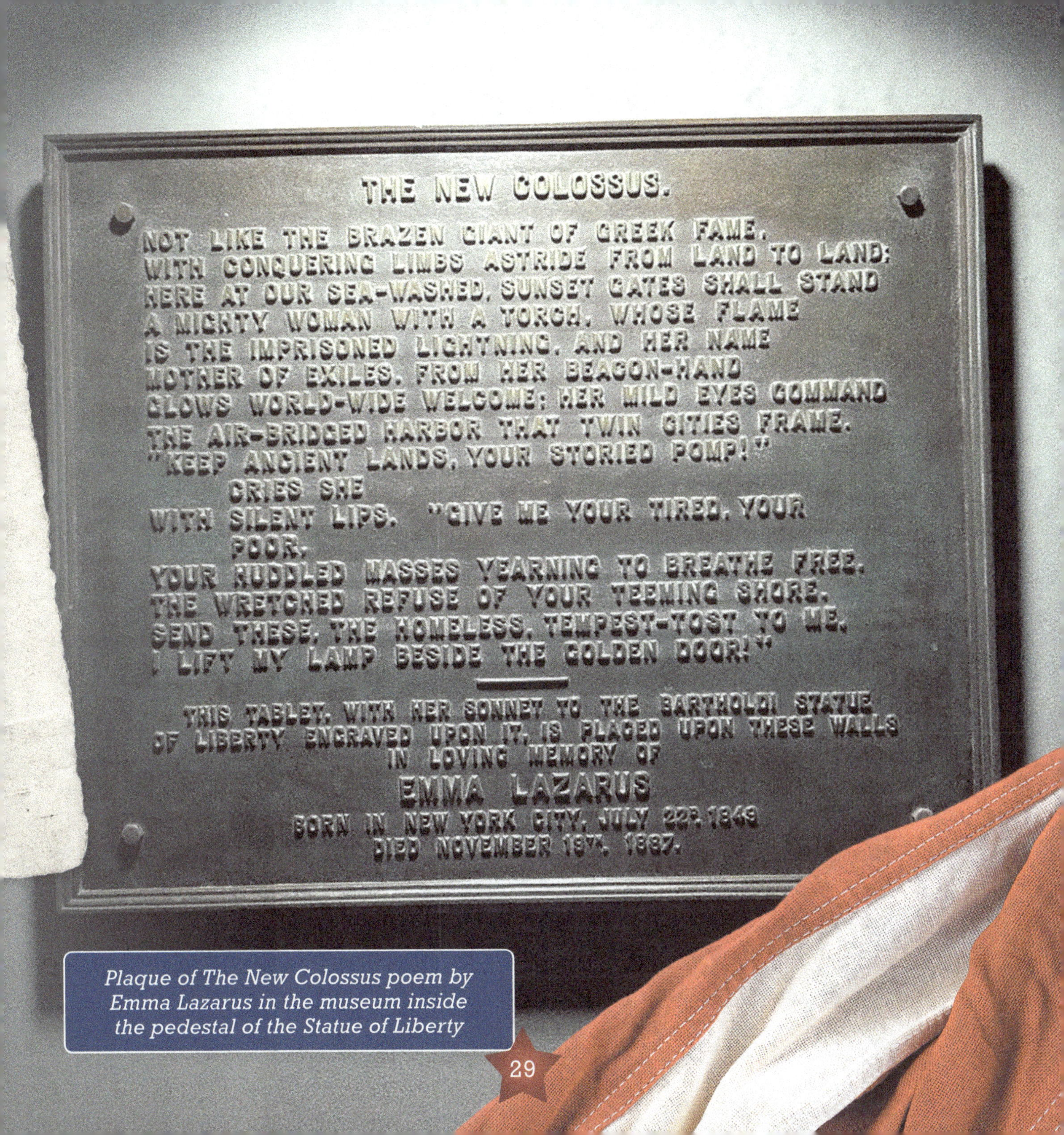
THE NEW COLOSSUS.
NOT LIKE THE BRAZEN GIANT OF GREEK FAME,
WITH CONQUERING LIMBS ASTRIDE FROM LAND TO LAND;
HERE AT OUR SEA-WASHED, SUNSET GATES SHALL STAND
A MIGHTY WOMAN WITH A TORCH, WHOSE FLAME
IS THE IMPRISONED LIGHTNING, AND HER NAME
MOTHER OF EXILES. FROM HER BEACON-HAND
GLOWS WORLD-WIDE WELCOME; HER MILD EYES COMMAND
THE AIR-BRIDGED HARBOR THAT TWIN CITIES FRAME.
"KEEP ANCIENT LANDS, YOUR STORIED POMP!"
CRIES SHE
WITH SILENT LIPS. "GIVE ME YOUR TIRED, YOUR
POOR,
YOUR HUDDLED MASSES YEARNING TO BREATHE FREE,
THE WRETCHED REFUSE OF YOUR TEEMING SHORE.
SEND THESE, THE HOMELESS, TEMPEST-TOST TO ME,
I LIFT MY LAMP BESIDE THE GOLDEN DOOR!"
THIS TABLET, WITH HER SONNET TO THE BARTHOLDI STATUE
OF LIBERTY ENGRAVED UPON IT, IS PLACED UPON THESE WALLS
IN LOVING MEMORY OF
EMMA LAZARUS
BORN IN NEW YORK CITY, JULY 22ND 1849
DIED NOVEMBER 19TH, 1887.

Plaque of The New Colossus poem by Emma Lazarus in the museum inside the pedestal of the Statue of Liberty

Pedestal for Bartholdi's Statue of Liberty on Bedloe's Island, New York Harbor

The statue was not made in America. It was a present from the French people. It was meant to honor the friendship between the countries. It was designed by Frédéric-Auguste Bartholdi. He was a sculptor. The workers in France finished the statue in 1884. After it was finished, the statue was taken apart. The pieces were sent to the United States. The pieces were put back together there.

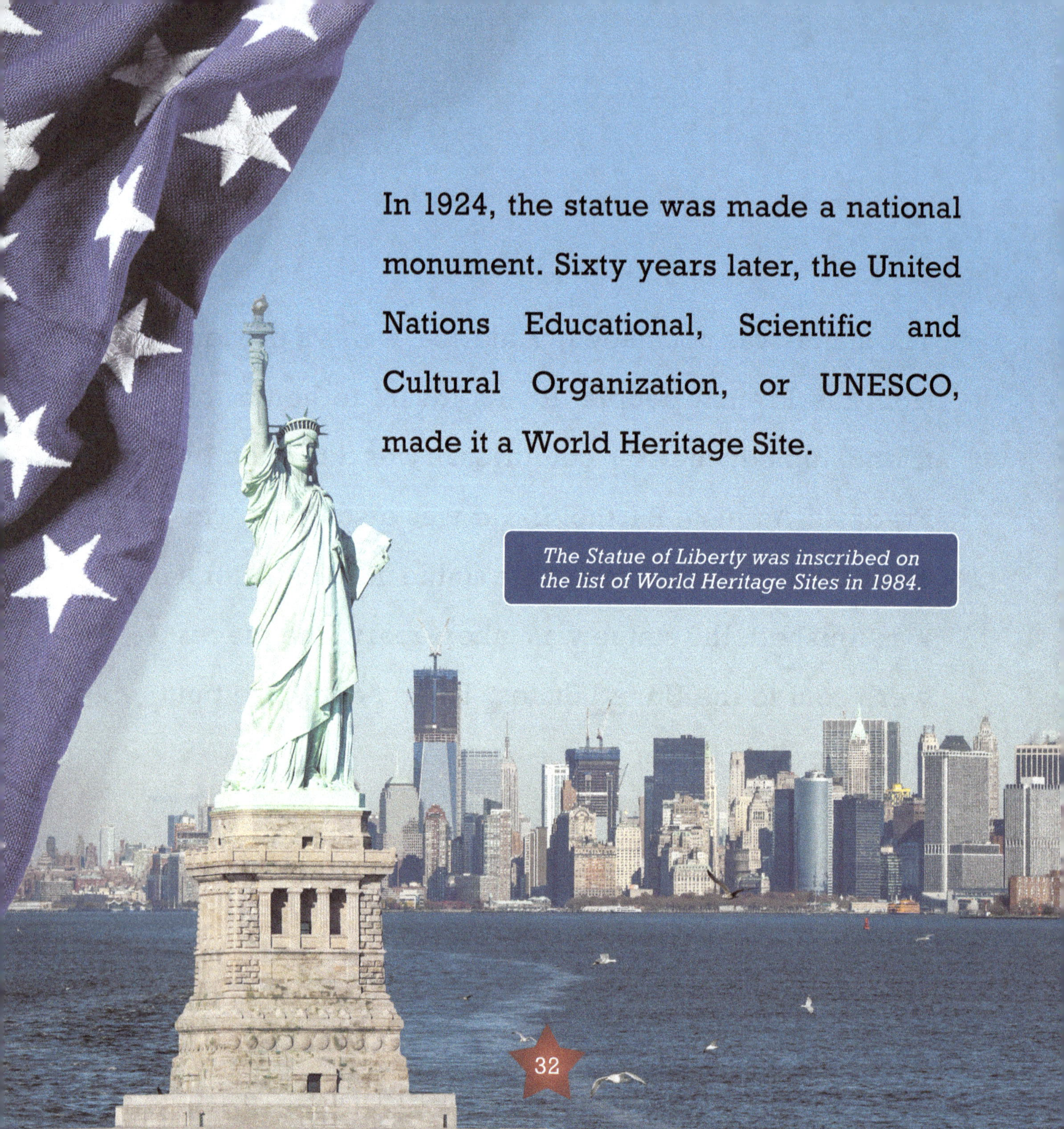

In 1924, the statue was made a national monument. Sixty years later, the United Nations Educational, Scientific and Cultural Organization, or UNESCO, made it a World Heritage Site.

The *Statue of Liberty* was inscribed on the list of World Heritage Sites in 1984.

Workers fixed the statue up in 1986. This was for its 100th birthday. A museum has also been opened. It is at the base of the statue.

CHAPTER TWO
OUR GOVERNMENT IN WASHINGTON D.C.

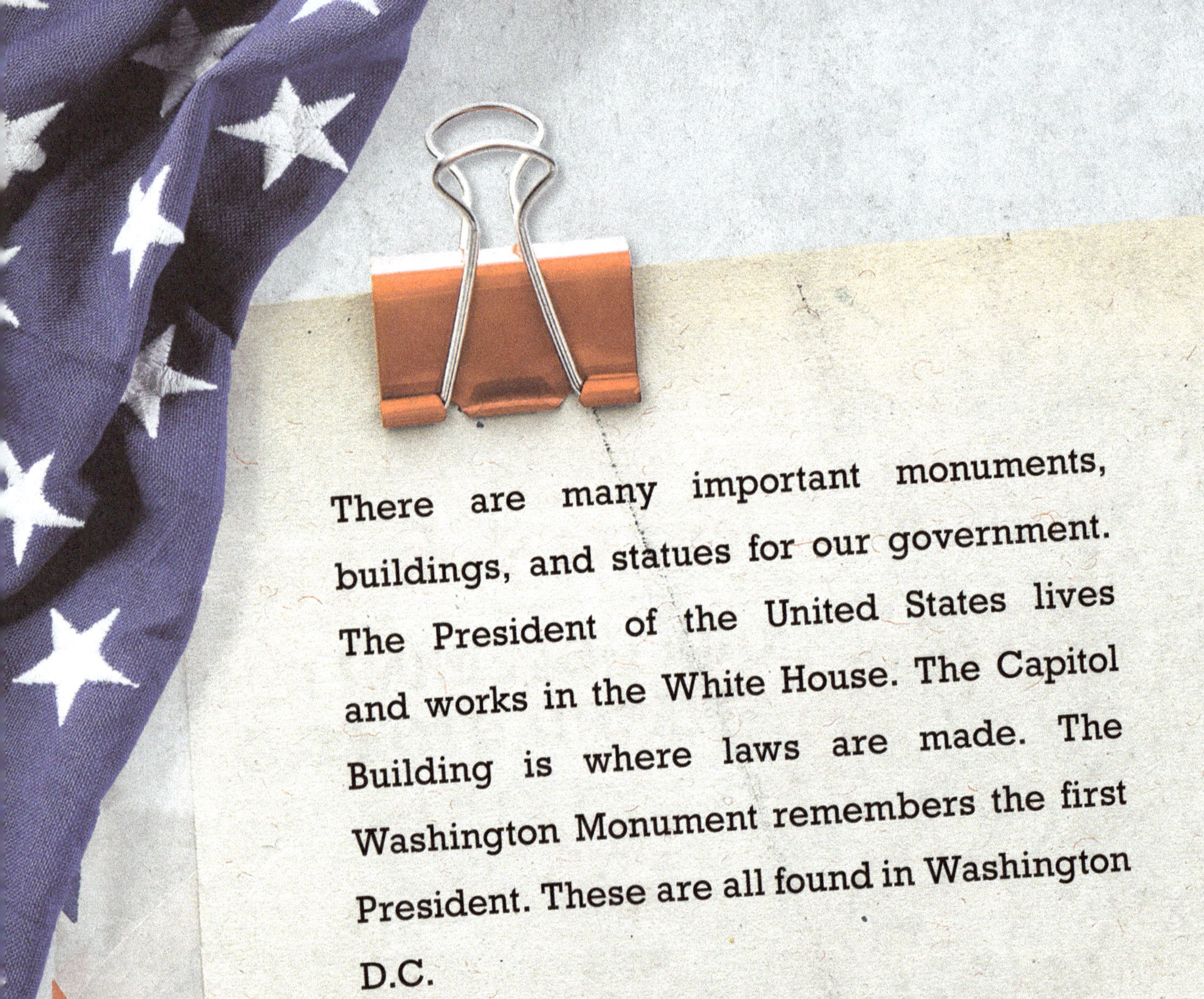

There are many important monuments, buildings, and statues for our government. The President of the United States lives and works in the White House. The Capitol Building is where laws are made. The Washington Monument remembers the first President. These are all found in Washington D.C.

An illustration of the important monuments and buldings in Washington DC

37

THE WHITE HOUSE

The White House is on 1600, Pennsylvania Avenue N.W. The walls are made of sandstone. These walls are painted white.

The White House, Washington DC

The first President did not live in the White House. He did not live in Washington D.C. either. They did not exist yet! The original capital was New York City. Later, it was moved to Philadelphia. In 1790, it was moved to Washington D.C.

A capital city is usually where the main government offices are. The capital of a country is where the country's leader works. This is where the laws for the entire country get made. States can have capital cities too. This is where the laws for the state are made. For example, the capital city of New York is Albany.

NEW YORK

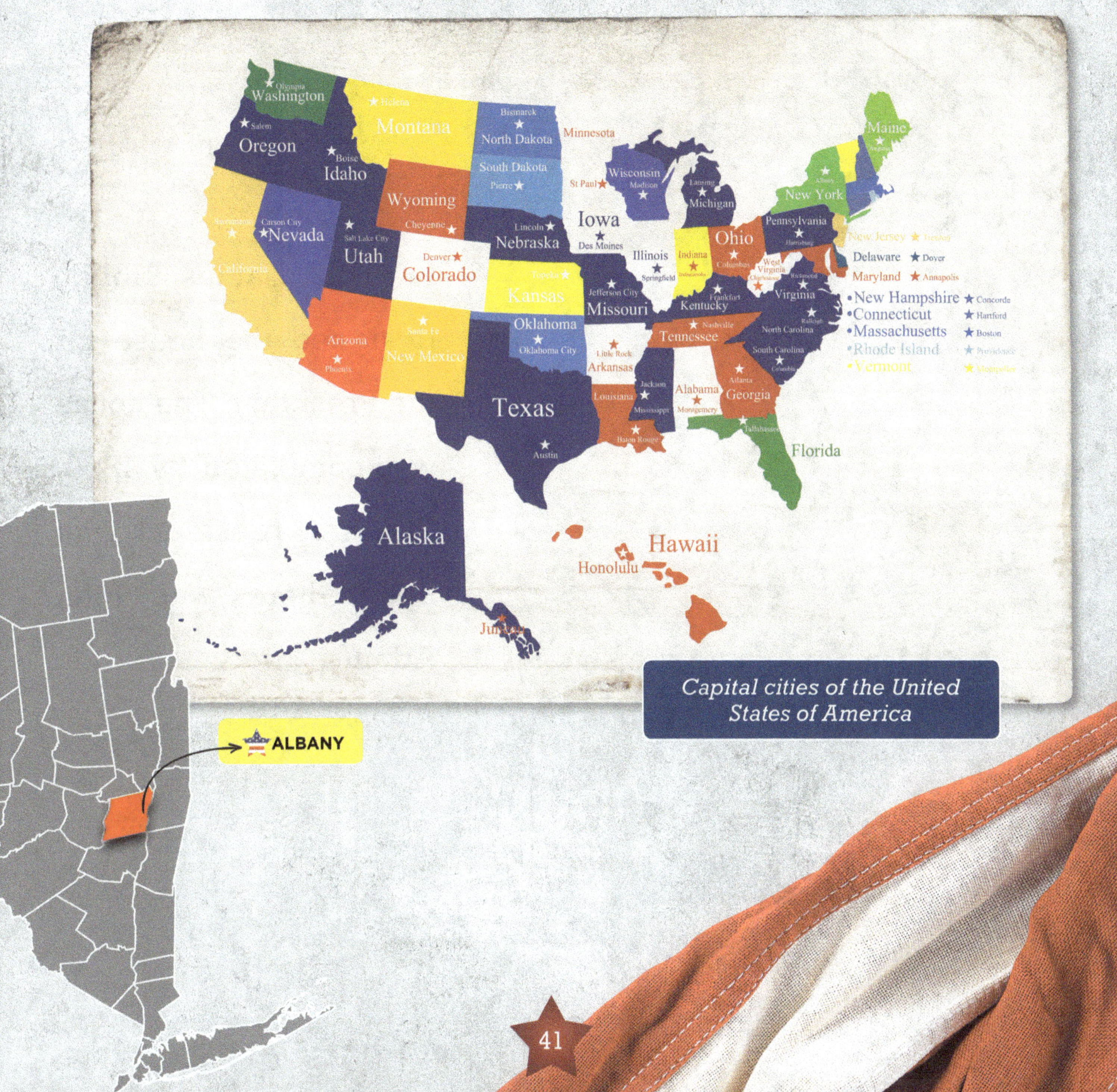

Olympia
Washington
Salem
Oregon
Helena
Montana
Bismarck
North Dakota
Minnesota
St Paul
Wisconsin
Madison
Lansing
Michigan
Maine
Augusta
Boise
Idaho
South Dakota
Pierre
New York
Albany
Wyoming
Cheyenne
Lincoln
Nebraska
Des Moines
Iowa
Illinois
Springfield
Ohio
Columbus
Pennsylvania
Harrisburg
New Jersey
Trenton
Sacramento
Carson City
Nevada
Salt Lake City
Utah
Denver
Colorado
Topeka
Kansas
Jefferson City
Missouri
Indiana
Indianapolis
West Virginia
Charleston
Richmond
Virginia
Frankfort
Kentucky
Delaware
Dover
Maryland
Annapolis
California
Arizona
Phoenix
Santa Fe
New Mexico
Oklahoma
Oklahoma City
Little Rock
Arkansas
Tennessee
Nashville
Raleigh
North Carolina
South Carolina
Columbia
New Hampshire
Concorde
Connecticut
Hartford
Massachusetts
Boston
Rhode Island
Providence
Vermont
Montpelier
Texas
Austin
Jackson
Mississippi
Louisiana
Baton Rouge
Alabama
Montgomery
Atlanta
Georgia
Tallahassee
Florida
Alaska
Juneau
Honolulu
Hawaii
Capital cities of the United
States of America
ALBANY

James Hoban

In 1792, James Hoban designed the house for the President. The house was completed by 1800. The first president who lived there was John Adams.

There was a fire in the White House in 1814. It was set by British soldiers. This was during the War of 1812. Fortunately, workers repaired the damage by 1817.

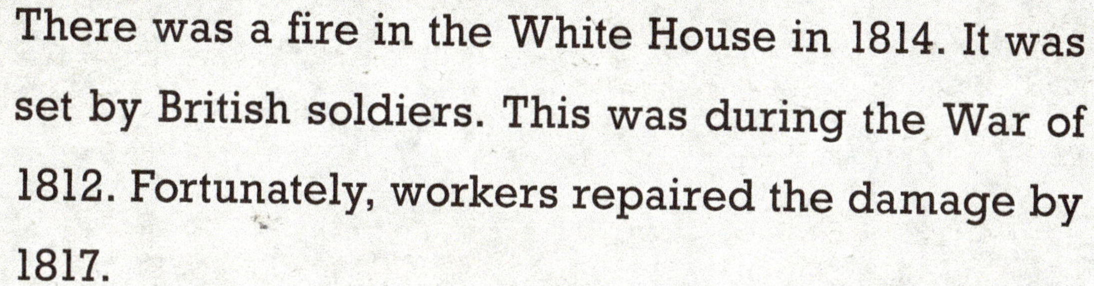
The British burned Washington, D.C., 200 years ago

There were some changes made in the 1900s. The West Wing was built for office space. The President's office is called the Oval Office.

The Vice President and government workers also have offices in the West Wing. The East Wing was also added for more space. It is where the First Lady and her staff have offices. The inside was changed too. The outside walls have never been changed. The public can tour some parts of the main building.

Some areas of the White House are used for events. The East room is used for large gatherings and dances. It is the biggest room.

The East Room, White House, Washington, D. C.

The State Dining Room is just a little bit smaller. 140 people can eat there! There are also the Red, Blue, and Green rooms. These are all on the first floor.

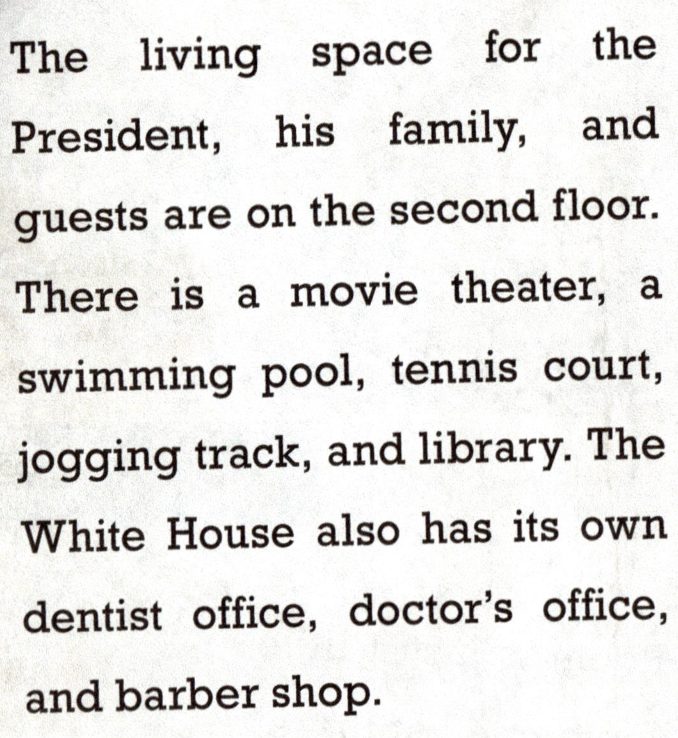

The living space for the President, his family, and guests are on the second floor. There is a movie theater, a swimming pool, tennis court, jogging track, and library. The White House also has its own dentist office, doctor's office, and barber shop.

Floor plan of the second floor of the White House

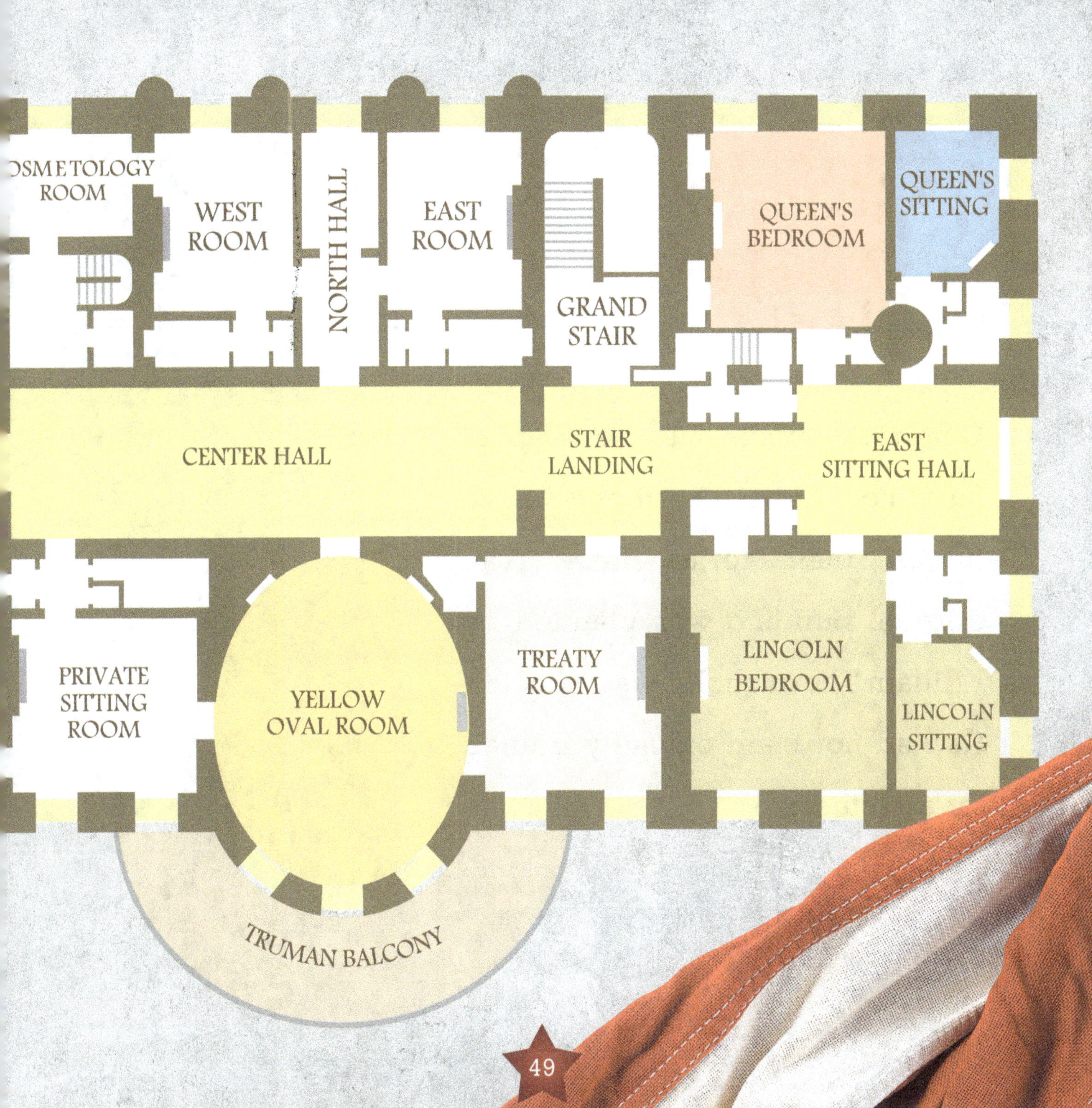
OSMETOLOGY ROOM
WEST ROOM
NORTH HALL
EAST ROOM
GRAND STAIR
QUEEN'S BEDROOM
QUEEN'S SITTING
CENTER HALL
STAIR LANDING
EAST SITTING HALL
PRIVATE SITTING ROOM
YELLOW OVAL ROOM
TREATY ROOM
LINCOLN BEDROOM
LINCOLN SITTING
TRUMAN BALCONY

THE CAPITOL BUILDING

Congress meets in the Capitol Building. Most presidents have begun their terms here. The original building was planned by William Thornton. He was a doctor. He had not been officially trained for architecture.

The Capitol Building is an impressive building. The dome is based on the dome of Saint Peter's Basilica. The top of the dome has a bronze statue. It is called *Freedom*.

President George Washington laid the corner stone on September 18, 1793.

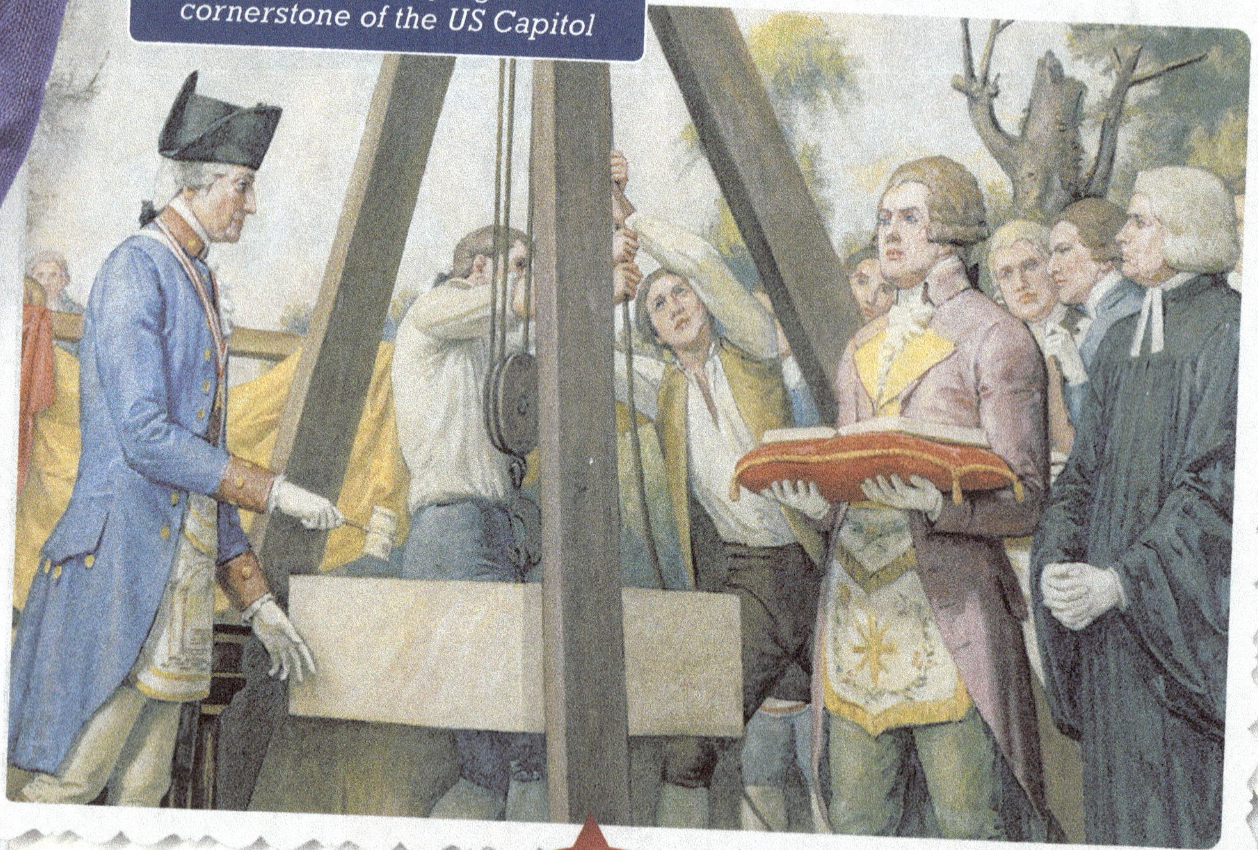

Washington laying the cornerstone of the US Capitol

The north wing was completed in 1800. It is where the Senate meets. The south wing was completed seven years later. It is where the House of Representatives meets.

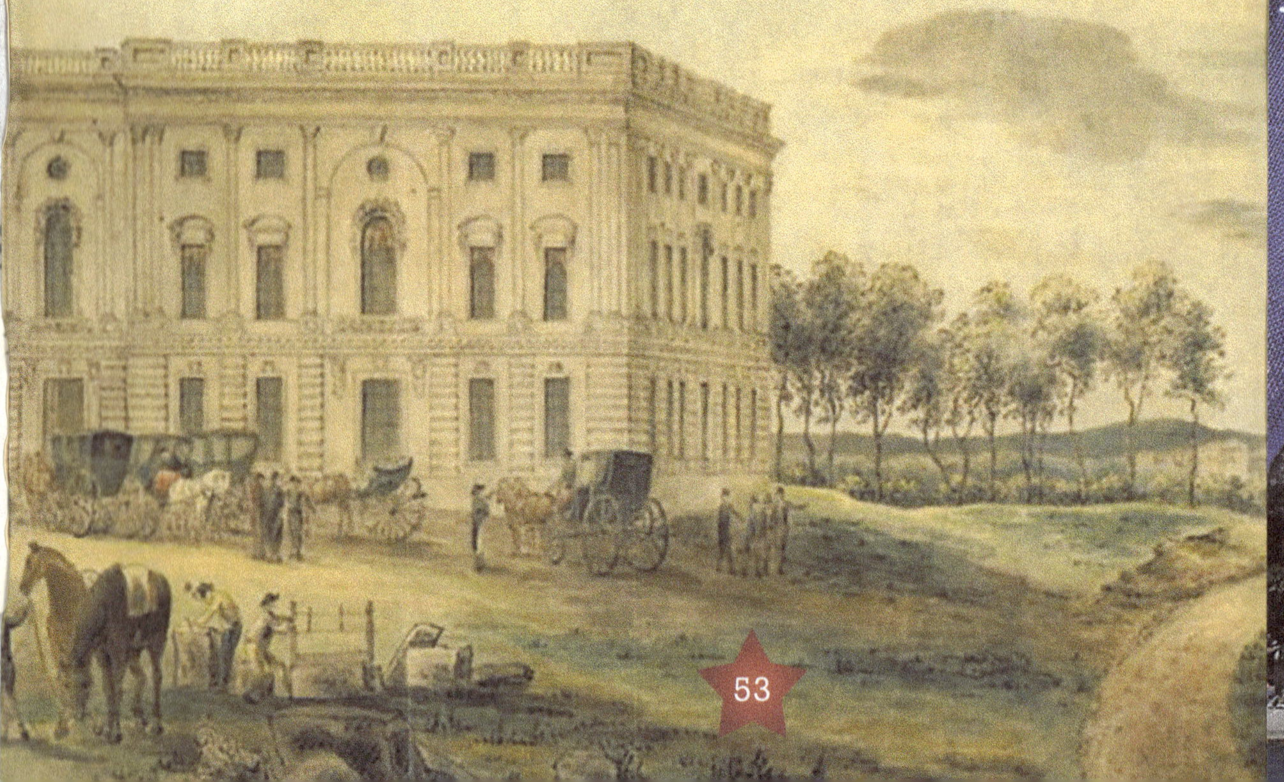

Completed northern wing of the Capitol

The Statue of Freedom

DID YOU KNOW?

Saint Peter's Basilica is one of the largest churches in the world. It was finished in 1626. This was over one hundred years after building began! The Basilica is in Vatican City. Vatican City is the smallest country in the world. It is ruled by the Pope of the Catholic Church.

St. Peter's Basilica, St. Peter's Square, Vatican City

The Apotheosis of Washington

The dome is over the Rotunda. This is a large room on the second floor. On the ceiling of the dome is a painting. It is called the Apotheosis of Washington. Apotheosis means someone becomes a god. It was painted by Constantino Brumidi. The painting shows Washington, gods and goddesses, and other American heroes.

Constantino Brumidi

Around the Rotunda there are also other paintings and statues. These show events from American history.

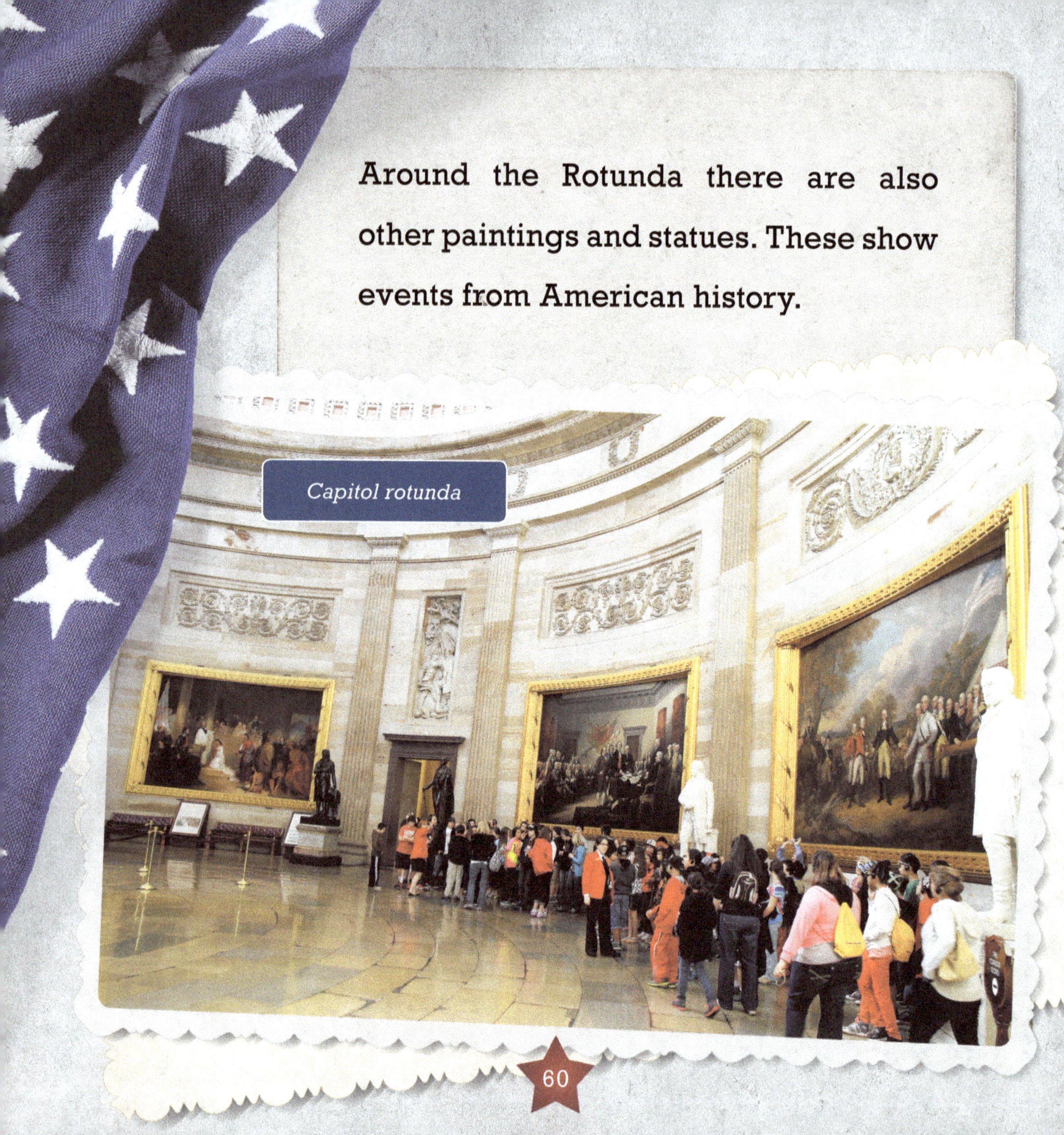

There is also a National Statuary Hall Collection. There are 100 statues there. There are two statues for all 50 states. The two statues are chosen for important people in that state's history.

The Capitol building
after the war of 1812

The Capitol Building was once looted and burned. This was also during the War of 1812. Luckily, there was a rainstorm. It kept the building from being destroyed entirely.

THE WASHINGTON MONUMENT

The Washington Monument used to be the tallest structure humans had ever built. This was when it was completed in 1884. The monument is almost 555 feet tall.

Washington Monument, Washington, D.C.

In 1833, The Washington National Monument Society chose the design. Robert Mills was the designer. He planned for the monument to be a 600-foot tall obelisk. An obelisk is a narrow pillar with a pyramid on top.

The building began in 1848. Unfortunately, there were many problems. The design had to change a lot. Finally, money ran out in 1854. The construction was halted.

In 1876, construction began again. The Army Corps of Engineers took over the project. They could not find stones that were the same color. It had just been too long. That is why the Washington Monument has three colors.

The partially completed Washington Monument.

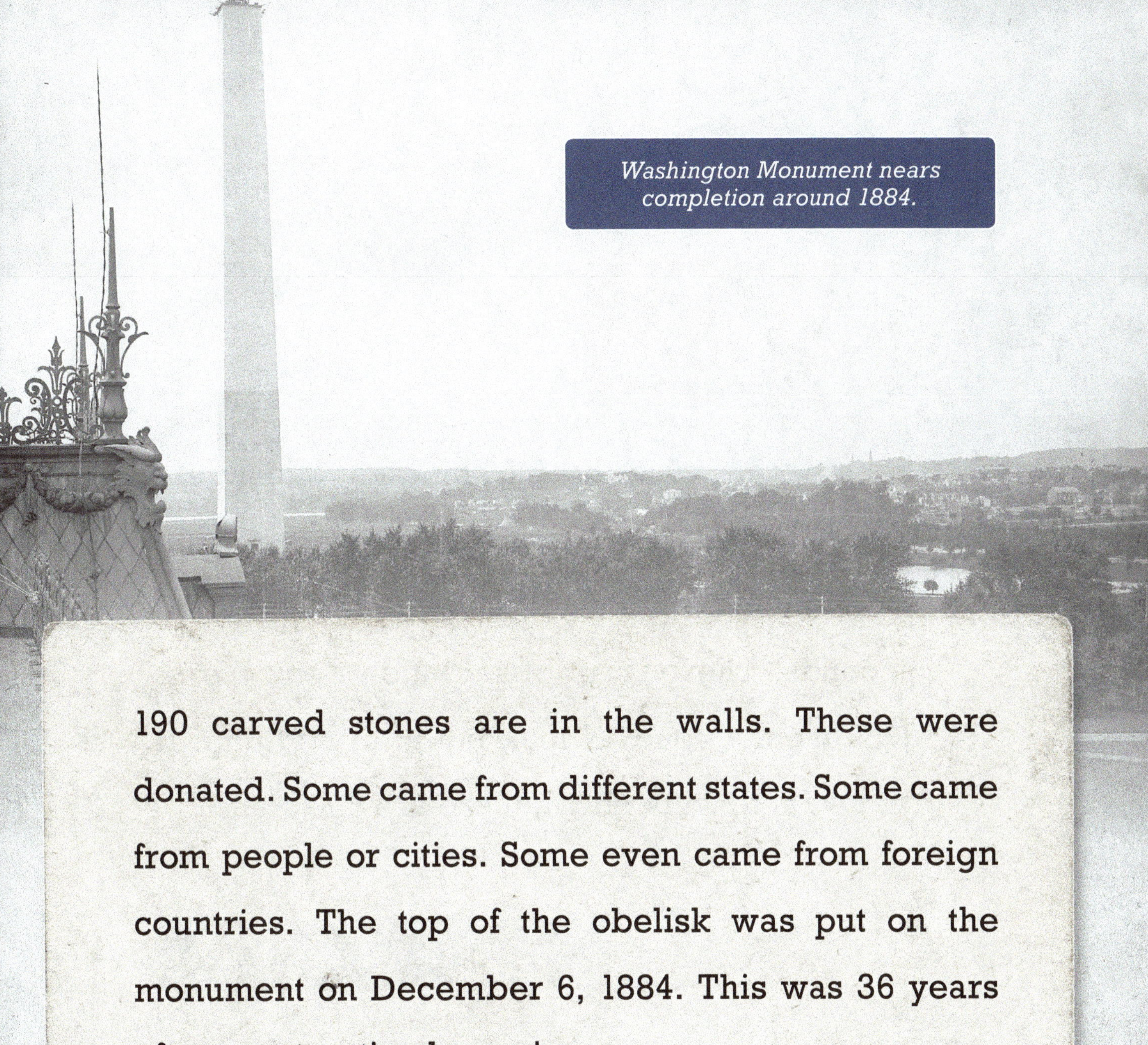

190 carved stones are in the walls. These were donated. Some came from different states. Some came from people or cities. Some even came from foreign countries. The top of the obelisk was put on the monument on December 6, 1884. This was 36 years after construction began!

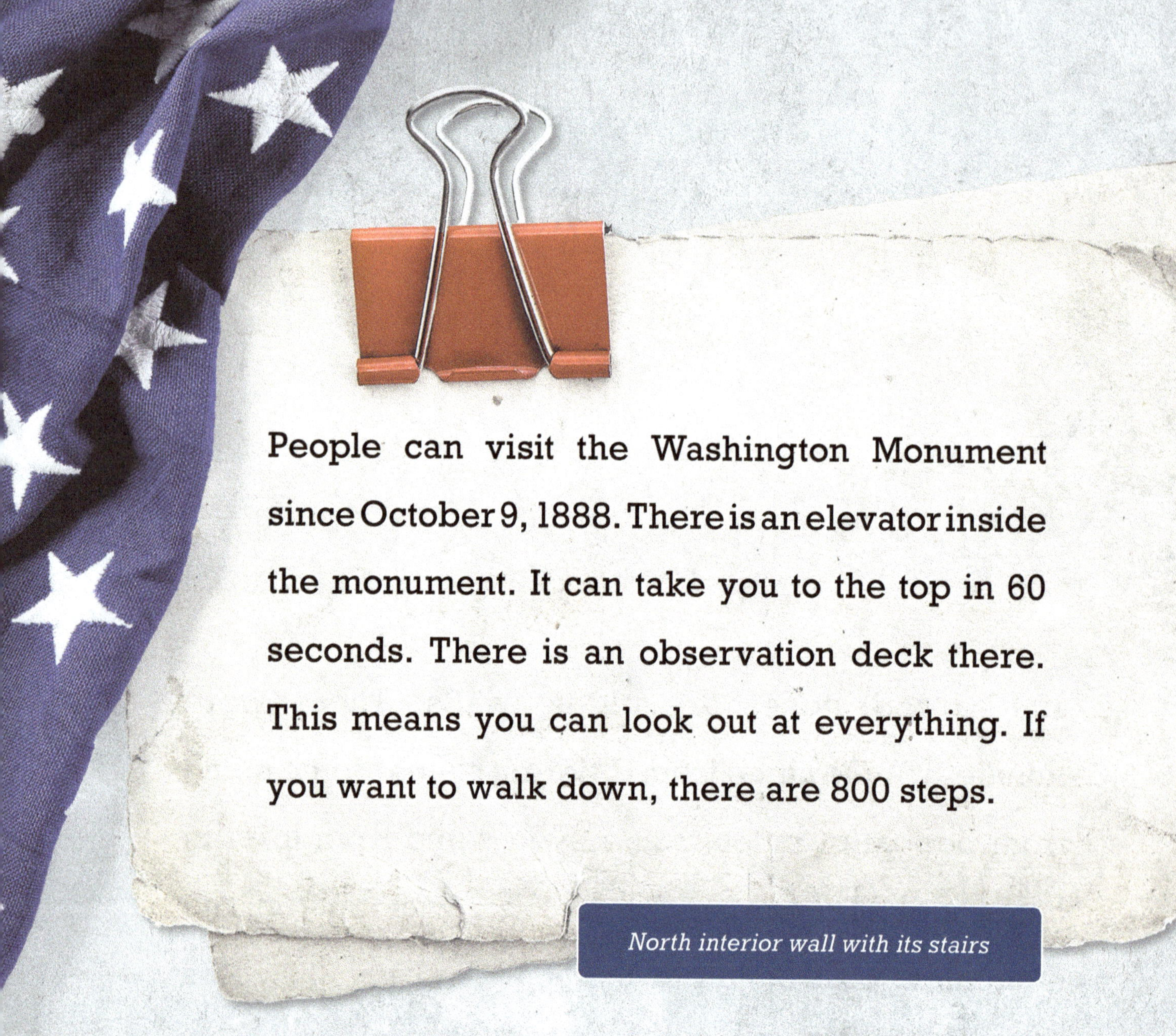

People can visit the Washington Monument since October 9, 1888. There is an elevator inside the monument. It can take you to the top in 60 seconds. There is an observation deck there. This means you can look out at everything. If you want to walk down, there are 800 steps.

North interior wall with its stairs

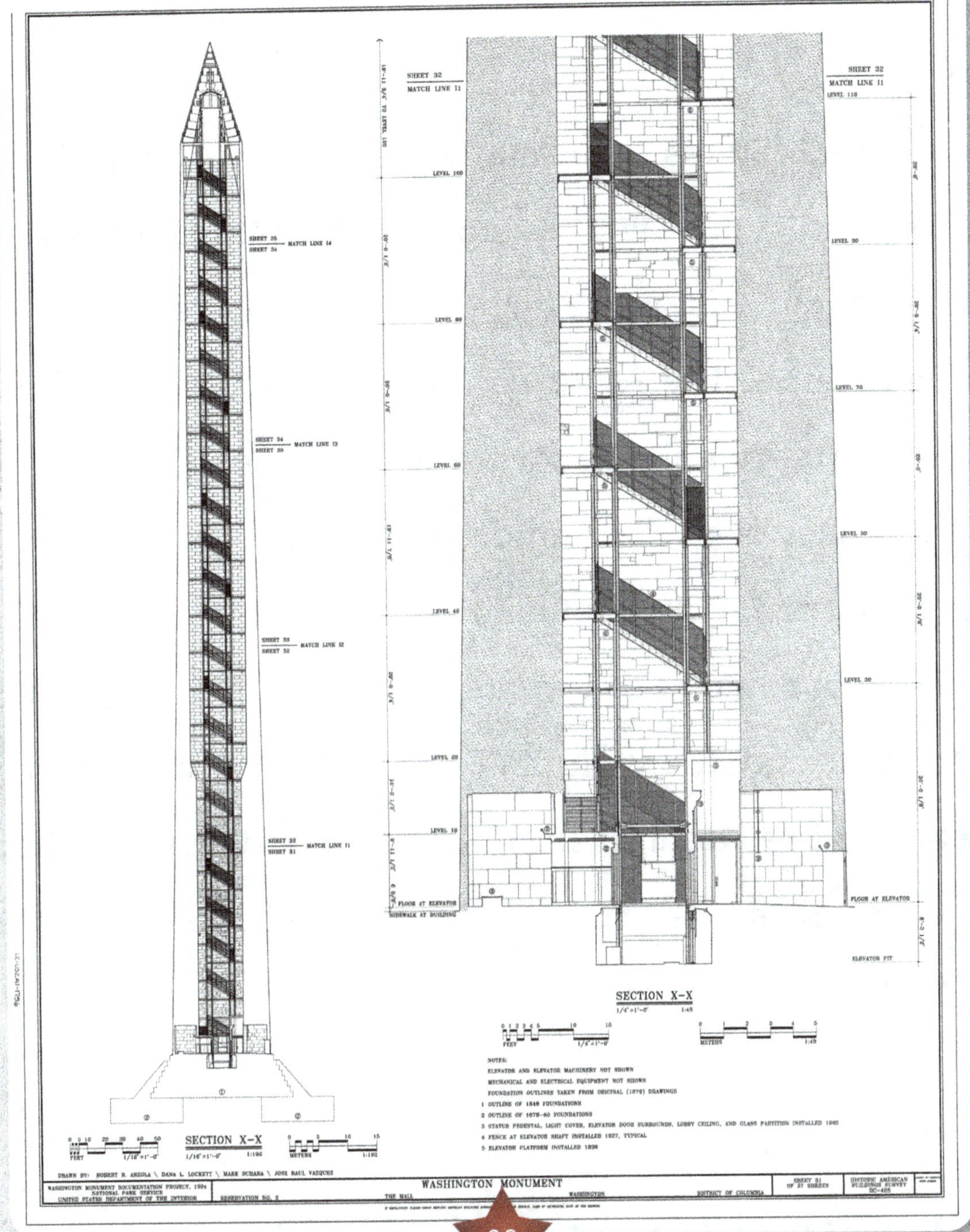

SHEET 32
MATCH LINE 11
SHEET 32
MATCH LINE 11
SHEET 35
SHEET 34 — MATCH LINE 14
SHEET 34 — MATCH LINE 13
SHEET 33
SHEET 33 — MATCH LINE 12
SHEET 32
SHEET 32 — MATCH LINE 11
SHEET 31
LEVEL 100
LEVEL 90
LEVEL 80
LEVEL 70
LEVEL 60
LEVEL 50
LEVEL 40
LEVEL 30
LEVEL 20
LEVEL 10
FLOOR AT ELEVATOR
SIDEWALK AT BUILDING
LEVEL 110
LEVEL 90
LEVEL 70
LEVEL 50
LEVEL 30
FLOOR AT ELEVATOR
ELEVATOR PIT
SECTION X-X
1/6"=1'-0"   1:48
FEET
METERS
SECTION X-X
1/16"=1'-0"   1/16"=1'-0"   1:192
FEET
METERS   1:192
NOTES:
ELEVATOR AND ELEVATOR MACHINERY NOT SHOWN
MECHANICAL AND ELECTRICAL EQUIPMENT NOT SHOWN
FOUNDATION OUTLINES TAKEN FROM ORIGINAL (1879) DRAWINGS
1 OUTLINE OF 1848 FOUNDATIONS
2 OUTLINE OF 1878-80 FOUNDATIONS
3 STATUE PEDESTAL, LIGHT COVER, ELEVATOR DOOR SURROUNDS, LOBBY CEILING, AND GLASS PARTITION INSTALLED 1963
4 FENCE AT ELEVATOR SHAFT INSTALLED 1927, TYPICAL
5 ELEVATOR PLATFORM INSTALLED 1936
DRAWN BY: ROBERT R. ARZOLA \ DANA L. LOCKETT \ MARK SCHARA \ JOSE RAUL VAZQUEZ
WASHINGTON MONUMENT DOCUMENTATION PROJECT, 1994
NATIONAL PARK SERVICE
UNITED STATES DEPARTMENT OF THE INTERIOR
RESERVATION NO. 2
THE MALL
WASHINGTON MONUMENT
WASHINGTON
DISTRICT OF COLUMBIA
SHEET 31
OF 37 SHEETS
HISTORIC AMERICAN
BUILDINGS SURVEY
DC-428

The United States has many monuments, buildings, statues, and symbols. They help us remember important things in our history. They are also where important things happen. The American flag is a symbol for all the States of America, its history, and its values. The Liberty Bell reminds of us the importance of the Declaration of Independence. The Statue of Liberty reminds us that anyone can come to America and be free. It also reminds us of our friendship with the French. The White House is where our President lives. The Capitol Building is where our laws are made. The Washington Monument honors our first President.

Visit

www.speedypublishing.com

To view and download free content on your favorite subject and browse
our catalog of new and exciting books for readers of all ages.